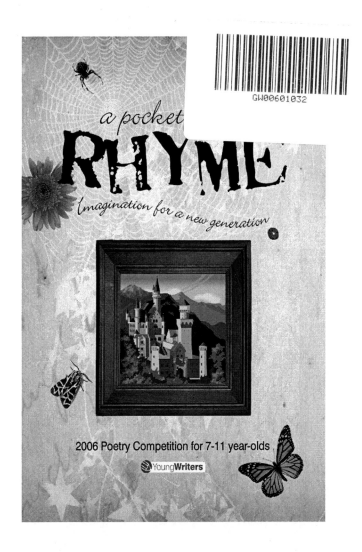

a pocket
RHYME
Imagination for a new generation

2006 Poetry Competition for 7-11 year-olds

YoungWriters

Pint-Sized Poets Vol I
Edited by Carrie Ghazanfer

 Young**Writers**

First published in Great Britain in 2006 by:
Young Writers
Remus House
Coltsfoot Drive
Peterborough
PE2 9JX
Telephone: 01733 890066
Website: www.youngwriters.co.uk

SB ISBN 1 84602 495 1

Foreword

Young Writers was established in 1991 and has been passionately devoted to the promotion of reading and writing in children and young adults ever since. The quest continues today. Young Writers remains as committed to the nurturing of poetic and literary talent as ever.

This year's Young Writers competition has proven as vibrant and dynamic as ever and we are delighted to present a showcase of the best poetry from across the UK and in some cases overseas. Each poem has been selected from a wealth of *A Pocketful Of Rhyme* entries before ultimately being published in this, our fourteenth primary school poetry series.

Once again, we have been supremely impressed by the overall quality of the entries we have received. The imagination, energy and creativity which has gone into each young writer's entry made choosing the poems a challenging and often difficult but ultimately hugely rewarding task - the general high standard of the work submitted ensured this opportunity to bring their poetry to a larger appreciative audience.

We sincerely hope you are pleased with this final collection and that you will enjoy *A Pocketful Of Rhyme Pint-Sized Poets Vol I* for many years to come.

Contents

Lyndon Green Junior School, Birmingham

Josh Hughes (7)	33
Conor Breeze (7)	34
Nicole Beagrie (8)	35
Lucy Hubble & Rebecka Barwood (8)	36
Daisy Andrews (8)	37
Oliver Dunlea (8)	38
Emma Smith (8)	39
Breton Busst (8)	40
Sophie Kirk (8)	41
Daniel Carr (8)	42
Skye Baker (8)	43
Hannah Thompson (9)	44
Mercedes Shelley (8)	45
Emma Warwood (8)	46
Bethan Machray (8)	47
Sophie Simmons (9)	48
Sarah Hinckley (9)	49
Rebecca Jones (10)	50
Emma Fitzgerald (11)	51
Rhiannon Satterley (10)	52
Lily Bennett (10)	53
Stephanie Beech (10)	54
Heather Pope (10)	55
Sophie Wills (11)	56
Molly Dewell (10)	57
Emily Mansell (10)	58
Bilal Ahmed (10)	59
Matthew Hoskin (10)	60
Jordan Bond (10)	61
Lauren Gallagher (11)	62
Daniel Hans (11)	63
Laura Russell (10)	64

Perry Court Junior School, Bristol

Danny Hawkins (10)	65
Anna McDougall	66
Georgiana Carnevale (11)	67
Shannon Jenkinson	68
Sophie Jackson (10)	69
Nathan Rickard (11)	70

Rebecca Higgins (10)	103
Abbie Tuffin (9)	104
Abigail Whittington (10)	105
Harry Smith (9)	106
Joe Alemzadeh (9)	107
April Buxton (10)	108
Ashley Davey (10)	109

Victoria College Preparatory School, Jersey

Peter Graham (10)	110
Oliver Colston-Weeks (11)	111
Harry Reid (10)	112
Rowan Spencer (11)	113
James Logue (10)	114
William Millar (11)	115
Bradley Gibb (10)	116
Fionn Douthwaite (11)	117
Cameron Stables (10)	118
Cyril Favre (10)	119
John du Heaume (10)	120
Jonny Falle (11)	121
Liam O'Regan (11)	122
Frankie de la Cour (11)	123
Hugo Barette (11)	124
Louis Sangan (10)	125
Francois Thebault (11)	126
Cameron Monro (10)	127
Struan Moore (11)	128
Jonny Singleton (11)	129
Joshua McGowan (11)	130
Luke Philpott (10)	131
Dominic Hirani (10)	132
Tanguy Tomes (10)	133
Stephen Coelho (10)	134
Chris Minchington (11)	135
Brad Morgan (11)	136
Graeme Overton (11)	137
Austen Colback (11)	138
Cameron McLean (11)	139
Joseph Asplet (10)	140
George Minty (11)	141

Wolf Fields Primary School, Norwood Green

The Poems

Sea Trip

I bet you don't know what it's like to be busted
To be unloved and just not trusted.
Here is the story; on the 21st of May,
I was off on holiday.
I was bored, I didn't know what to do,
I caught sight of a beach with a boat, brand new.

As I raced forwards, I hurt my shin,
But I didn't care, I climbed right in.
It was made of smooth pine wood,
I started rowing as fast as I could,
Quickly towards the horizon,
Peering up at the beautiful sun.

The police came, I wasn't authorised,
They locked me up, I *was* surprised
And now I am behind cell bars
And now I think, I'll stick to cars.

Katy Summers (10)

Light And Dark

Sunshine, moonlight,
Stars shine bright.
Light by day,
Dark by night.
Lucky me to have my sight,
That's all we have tonight.

Harry Burgan (10)

Romance

Romance is the colour red, like a big heart beating every second.
Romance sounds like little golden bells, chiming throughout the day.
Romance tastes like sweet strawberry candyfloss on a hot
summer's day.
Romance smells like fresh country air, swaying my hair from
side to side.
Romance looks like thousands of hearts, all together and ready
to burst with laughter.
Romance feels like a soft pillow ready to be jumped on and being
slept on until the morning.
Romance reminds me of Valentine's Day, when we give our
true love something
And you will love them until your hearts are filled with happiness!

Keely Fellows (10)
Beauty Bank Primary School, Stourbridge

Sadness

Sadness is the colour of watery tears.
Sadness sounds like a thousand people in pain.
Sadness tastes like tears dripping in my mouth.
Sadness smells like hearts, broken into bits.
Sadness looks like a butterfly dying.
Sadness feels like my heart is shattering.
Sadness reminds me of *death!*

Terri Johnson (10)
Beauty Bank Primary School, Stourbridge

Fear - A Nightmare That Never Goes!

Fear is the kind of colour that I cannot describe, it hums around me,
disturbing me.
Fear sounds like a chainsaw, scraping and digging into my flesh
and then retracting.
Fear tastes like blood coming from a fresh human heart.
Fear smells like rats scratching and scurrying, looking for food.
Fear looks like dead bodies, waiting to come alive.
Fear feels like a nightmare - never stopping, never going.
Fear reminds me of ghosts coming to haunt me, trying to scare me.

Iqra Khalid (10)
Beauty Bank Primary School, Stourbridge

Sadness

Sadness is the colour of the deep blue sea.
Sadness sounds like clean water running down as fast as possible
                                              into your mouth.
Sadness smells like the blue open seas with fish sweeping in and out
                                              of your toes.
Sadness looks like people on their own in the longest place
                                              on the planet.
Sadness feels like you're stranded in the middle of nowhere with
                                              no one to hug.
Sadness reminds me of the lonely people on the planet and no one
                                              to look out to.

Matthew Willetts (11)
Beauty Bank Primary School, Stourbridge

Fear

Fear is black and red mixed together.
Fear sounds like a beat of a heart slowing down.
Fear tastes like rotten beer.
Fear smells like a very wet cave that's been there for years.
Fear looks like a black abyss opening in the centre of the ocean.
Fear feels like an arrow that has gone right through you.
Fear reminds me of death.

Lee Russon (10)
Beauty Bank Primary School, Stourbridge

Fear

Fear is the colour black, like a blinded eye in the middle of nowhere.
Fear sounds like a black soul, fighting its way to the centre of the Earth
Like a big ball of fire.
Fear tastes like frightened souls inside my heart.
Fear smells like black tar in the centre of the Earth.
Fear looks like one dark soul under the earth.
Fear feels like the icy dead sea when its darkness falls towards the
Earth and sun.
Fear reminds me of souls and the black widow.

Lewis Hackett (11)
Beauty Bank Primary School, Stourbridge

Mr Evil

Mr Evil was a deathly dark demon.
His wings were grey and stone!
He was more powerful than the heavenly gods.
His claws were razor-sharp and could rip down a building.
Under his black, gold-trimmed armour laid only souls and dust!
In his house was a dark abyss that opened the gateway to Hell!
He was a deadly nightly nightmare.
His muscles could out-beat the world with one touch.
He could cast raging red lightning out of his claws.
Dark dragon-raging flames were covering his eyes.

He lived in a black wood filled with deathly demons.
The trees were dead and decayed.
The sky always stayed in rage, blackness and ghostly souls.

Wherever he was, an earthquake tremor shook the world!
He had infinite power and could never be killed.
Every day he would search for demons and rip them apart with his claws
Taking their bodies and throwing them in the trapdoor to Hell!

People from the nearby town would always hear crying deaths.
In the night, when the dark grey moon was falling,
Everyone was sure they could see his beastly red eyes scanning the town
Like a camera on top of the tall, towering, dead trees.
Did he have any friends?
Did he have a good side?
Nobody knew . . .

Jack Walker (11)
Beauty Bank Primary School, Stourbridge

Love

Love is as soft as a cuddly brown teddy.
Love is like a dream, when you're sleeping deeply.
Love smells like a sweet-scented perfume.
Love smells like a falling petal from a red rose.
Love feels like butterflies gently tickling your tummy.
Love feels like the softness of a feather.
Love tastes like soft marshmallows toasting on a fire.
Love tastes like a freshly baked birthday cake.
Love looks like children playing happily at the park.
Love looks like clouds floating across a pale blue sky.
Love sounds like the first birds singing sweetly in the morning.
Love sounds like a harp being played peacefully.
Love is as quiet as a ladybird's wings fluttering.
Love is like the sunrise on a bright new day.

Daniel Taylor (10)
Beauty Bank Primary School, Stourbridge

Love Is A Dream

Love is a dream that I think of throughout the night.
Love is a dream, I shout with all my might.
Love is a dream like the rosebuds that open.
Love is a dream like the tropical oceans.
Love is a dream like a cream pearl in an oyster shell.
Love is a dream like the sound of a ringing bell.
Love is a dream like a freshly baked cake.
Love is a dream like a flowing lake.
Love is a dream like the scent of perfume.
Love is a dream that will never hurt you.
Love is a dream like the sight of a newborn baby.
Love is a dream like a dancing lady.
Love is a dream like that caring feeling.
Love is a dream when my heart's healing.

Love can't be a dream, but that's how it seems.
It's only around the corner, waiting for her.

Esha Norris (10)
Beauty Bank Primary School, Stourbridge

The Dragon Boat Race

The water is calm and still.
People patiently wait with curiosity on who's going to win.
The smell of salty air is blowing in everybody's faces.

And then . . . they're off!
Away!

The oars splash through the water.
The boats swiftly overtake each other.
They build up tremendous speed.
The finish line is in sight.
Finally they finish.
Happily the winning team get out of the boat,
With sounds of applause all around.

Ellen Partridge (9)
Dudley Wood Primary School, Dudley

Dragon Boat Racing

The water is still and calm.
Fish are swimming peacefully.
The air is frozen in its place
And the audience are getting chatty
As a nervous group of men climb into their decorative boats!

And then . . . they're off!
Away!

The water is swish-swashing.
Worried fish are swimming left and right with all their might.
But the oars are holding them back!
A big gong is pounding,
Beating air comes rushing from the oars.
Men are getting sweaty and hot.
Their arms start to ache as they beat the water rapidly.
The finish line draws near
And our competition draws to an end.
Cheers are heard from the audience . . .
The red team have won!

Natarnya Walcott (9)
Dudley Wood Primary School, Dudley

The Dragon Boat Race

People impatiently waiting.
The deep water not moving a muscle.
The people whispering, 'What's going to happen?'
Legs shaking, people ready to shout.

And then . . . they're off!
Away!

The oars splashing,
Boats zooming away like cheetahs.
People cheering the boats on,
Who's going to win?
The green team have won!

Thomas Wall (8)
Dudley Wood Primary School, Dudley

Café

Eating the crispy but juicy bacon as it sizzles on my plate.
Eating hot burnt sausages covered in spicy sauce.
Eating a hot dog in a huge bap with crispy fried onions.
Eating double chocolate cookies and creamy ice cream.

Smelling the stale scent of the café.
Smelling the rich aroma of coffee.
Smelling the sizzling fat in a pan.
Smelling the spicy sausages cooking in the oven.

Hearing people chatting loudly.
Hearing wine glasses clinking.
Hearing knives chopping vegetables.
Hearing people in the rush hour.
Hearing newspapers rustling.

Seeing people eating big breakfasts.
Seeing big cakes with lots of decoration.
Seeing people drinking their coffee or latte.
Seeing big ice cream cones ready to be eaten.

Alice Aubrey (9)
Dudley Wood Primary School, Dudley

The Sun

Winter, I don't get the chance
To burn and carbonise.
The clouds block off my light beams,
So I try to grow in size.
If I can outgrow them, then you will see
My beams are really scorching,
Burning, destructive me!

Ivan Walcott (11)
Dudley Wood Primary School, Dudley

My Granny

My granny
is
loving,
kind
and promising.
She reminds me
of walks
and happy memories.

She reads books
sad books,
happy books
and
funny books
and all sorts.

She sits with me for
a
long
time.
Sewing and colouring
and other fun things.
She smells
like perfume.

She
is
the best
and only granny.
Always in my heart.
She is like a cake for everybody.

Phoebe Abrahams (8)
Freshford CE (VC) Primary School, Bath

My Brother

My brother
is like
an
untrained monkey
from
the zoo.

Like a dog
covered in
mud.

Like
a mad thing
from
nowhere.

An alien
from
outer
space.

My brother,
kind
of . . .
sweet.

Megan Ross   (8)
Freshford CE (VC) Primary School, Bath

My Brothers

They eat everything.
Packets of crisps
Baked beans and cold meat from Sunday.

Handfuls of food
In their mouths
And in the bin.

Every morning they come into my room
And tickle me until I *burst* into laughter
Or scream my head off.
They love playing rough with machines,
Until they break.

They are different,
Intelligent and read a lot
And do what they want.
Curly and straight,
Brown and golden-blonde.
Friendly grins, I-like-you smiles.
I love my brothers
And they love me.

Nell Robins (8)
Freshford CE (VC) Primary School, Bath

Philip

Very annoying,
he is quite fast,
messy and
very odd.
Funny,
loud,
good sometimes.
Small,
but cheeky.
He has crazy
long hair.
Likes pizza.
Plays games
with me,
like
Mousetrap.

Matthew Jacob (7)
Freshford CE (VC) Primary School, Bath

My Friend

My friend has
Muddy football boots
In the hall.
He is ace at
Computers.
Funny and silly.
He plays football with me.
He has a toothy smile
And tells football jokes.
He is always chasing presents
On the rooftops.

Harry Lisney (7)
Freshford CE (VC) Primary School, Bath

My Brother

My brother is
Very kind
Most of the time.
He is
Sometimes annoying,
But most of
The time he is very sweet.
Always there,
And never not.
He has silky brown
Hair.
He is
Such a TV fool.
He never
Stops.
He is
Sweet, but crazy
And he is
Always on the go.

Esme Williams (7)
Freshford CE (VC) Primary School, Bath

My Cousin Molly

Molly is like a warm hug,
Full of craziness.

Beautiful red
Lips,
Glossy
Brown hair,
Glittering
In the sun.

A cheeky
Monkey,
Incredibly clever,
A sitting down and standing up girl.

A sharing,
A cream bun kind of
Cousin.

Safia Hatton Smith (7)
Freshford CE (VC) Primary School, Bath

Elly

The queen
Of the
Dressing up clothes.

Six years
Old
And
Bossy.

She and I
Make
A pet shop
Full of
Lizards
And
Big cats.

She swims like a frog.
She is my cousin.

Charlie Palastre (8)
Freshford CE (VC) Primary School, Bath

She Is Fabulous

She is fabulous
In
The garden.

Understanding
In the
House.

All she needs
Is
A cup of tea
To come
And play
With me.

She is like a cake
In the kitchen.
Fire-making master.

I desire her,
As she
Is
Fond
Of me.

James Onyett (9)
Freshford CE (VC) Primary School, Bath

My Aunt Lou

My Aunt Lou is pretty and kind.
She always has a cheeky grin or smile.
I see her normally at my grandma's.
She loves the sunshine like I do
And maybe fizzy water for a treat.
She is fun.
She is pink, pink and pinker.
Dresses and tops, jeans and jackets and scarves
And just right for me.

Louisa Hunt (7)
Freshford CE (VC) Primary School, Bath

My Brother

Loves music,
Is very cool.
The best at football.

Goes into town with his friends.
Walks in the woods.
Plays with guns and swords.

Good at listening
And learning.

He
Loves food
And friends
And furry things
And
I love him.

Joseph Bodur (8)
Freshford CE (VC) Primary School, Bath

My Friend

He is careful
And
Very
Kind.

He likes the computer,
Santa's
Roof-hopping.

He is like ham pizza
With
Pineapple.

He is hiding
In a comic book.

He is laughing
With
Fish
And
Chips.

He is attracted to
The Beanos.

He is my friend.

Hayden Burton (7)
Freshford CE (VC) Primary School, Bath

My Mum

My mum is like high land
On top of a mountain.

She is always there.

She is in the hall
When you get in.

She makes a cup of tea
She sits down.

When she gets up
She goes into the garden.

Mum is home
And home is Mum.

Felix Maclaren (8)
Freshford CE (VC) Primary School, Bath

My Mum And Dad

My mum is sweet like a flower.
My dad is strong like an ox.

My mum is beautiful like a butterfly.
My dad works for England, he keeps the land.

Kind, sweet, loving mother and father.
Sparkles of love in their eyes.

Emily Brundrett (8)
Freshford CE (VC) Primary School, Bath

My Best Friend

He likes football.
He has muddy shoes, clothes,
Trousers, everything.

He loves the dog
And the dog jumps up at him.

He is the winner of *Burnout 2*
He says, 'Can I have one?'

He runs like I can't describe.
He is funny and lots of laughs.

Daniel Hancock (9)
Freshford CE (VC) Primary School, Bath

My Friend

Tough and cool,
Kind to his little brother.

Plays with me and Stanley,
He loves two dads.

He comes to mine,
I go to his.

Big field by the garden,
Cool home.

He loves . . .
Going to his dad's on Sundays,
His baby brother,
Pokémon
And helping
His mum.
Always in my head.

Ben Hancock (9)
Freshford CE (VC) Primary School, Bath

A Star On Mars

A star on Mars,
I've never seen a star on Mars,
Jars full of stars,
I've never seen a star on Mars
But everyone says it's true.

Josh Hughes (7)
Lyndon Green Junior School, Birmingham

My Fish

My fish is very big,
He's almost like a whale.
He has a huge fat tummy
And a big, gold, floppy tail.

I wonder what my fish
Dreams about at night?
When I am sleeping in my bed
And he is out of sight.

Maybe in his dreams,
He thinks he is a shark.
Scaring all the little fish,
Playing murder in the dark.

Other kids have cats and dogs,
But that is not my wish.
I wouldn't mind a pony,
But I really love my fish!

Conor Breeze (7)
Lyndon Green Junior School, Birmingham

I Didn't Mean To

I didn't mean to spill my milk
Or lose the front door key.
I didn't mean to kick the cat,
But you're always blaming me.

I didn't mean to come home late,
Mess my bedroom up, hurt myself
Or shout for help when I did not need it,
Now it's the last time to say
Sorry.

Nicole Beagrie (8)
Lyndon Green Junior School, Birmingham

I Didn't Mean It

I didn't mean to break the vase,
Smash the window or kick the cat.
I didn't mean to cut the new sofa,
Lose my homework sheet or break the computer wires.
I didn't mean to get a detention
By snapping the teacher's pen.
I didn't mean to blow up the microwave
And to kick the baby like a football.
I try to say *sorry* and still you don't accept it.

Lucy Hubble & Rebecka Barwood (8)
Lyndon Green Junior School, Birmingham

Springtime

Flowers in the garden, growing quietly all day long.
Listening to the sweet songs of the songbird.

The frogs are skipping in the pond,
Here come the animals from their long winter sleep.

We're planting the bulbs,
Hip hip hooray!
Let's watch the flowers grow today,
Springtime is on the way.
Hip hip hooray!

Daisy Andrews (8)
Lyndon Green Junior School, Birmingham

Hallowe'en

Hallowe'en is fun.
Hallowe'en is spooky.
Hallowe'en is full of ghosts.
Hallowe'en makes you *boogie*.

Witches fly up to the sky.
The mummies rise and rise.
The children shout and cry,
It's Hallowe'en tonight.

Oliver Dunlea (8)
Lyndon Green Junior School, Birmingham

Shooting Star

Once, when I looked out the window,
I saw a shooting star.,
I wished I was thirteen,
But the next day I was thirty!
And I had children
And I had a husband.
I screamed
And that night I had to change my girl's nappy,
It stank the house out!
And every night I looked for that shooting star
And I'll never forgive it.

Emma Smith (8)
Lyndon Green Junior School, Birmingham

The Lynx

The lynx's fur is grey like a pigeon
And it camouflages to stalk its prey, while moving quietly.
Its teeth are like daggers
And they purr really loud.
Also, they often eat fish.

Breton Busst (8)
Lyndon Green Junior School, Birmingham

A Spooky Night

Tonight is a night that's a spooky night.
Watch out that a ghost doesn't give you a fright.

It's dark, it's gloomy, it's frightful and scary.
Watch out for a goblin that's green and hairy.

There's witches on broomsticks all over the sky.
Whilst swarms of bats go fluttering by.

So that is the story about the spooky night.
Watch out that no one gives you a fright.
Boo!

Sophie Kirk (8)
Lyndon Green Junior School, Birmingham

In The Jungle

Down, down, deep in the jungle,
Where bananas and mangoes are grown.
If you listen carefully and stand on your tiptoes . . .
You may see monkeys swing past the hippos.

Down, down, deep in the jungle,
Where the sun is very hot.
You may hear the roar of a tiger,
Or could it be a big hairy spider?

Down, down, deep in the jungle,
Where it can be dark.
The trees are close together,
Watch out for bats and tiny ants
Running up the tree bark.

Down, down, deep in the jungle,
If you still want to go.
Who knows what you might see?
You'll never really know.

Daniel Carr (8)
Lyndon Green Junior School, Birmingham

My Sister

My sister is a pain in the bum.
She keeps on saying that she has won.
But no, not yet, she hasn't won.
Because it's my turn now and guess what I've done
I've put a little mouse in her bed.
'Argh!' She screams and shouts,
'Oh Mommy look, I've seen a mouse!'
She says to me, 'I've had enough and you are too tough
And I have had enough.' So *yippee*
That means that she is weak and I am glad that we're unique.

Skye Baker (8)
Lyndon Green Junior School, Birmingham

My Autumn Poem

Trees, trees, let down your leaves.
Don't you know it's autumn?
Wind, wind, blow your hardest.
The trees won't listen to me!

Green, orange, yellow and red,
Falling to the ground!

Hannah Thompson (9)
Lyndon Green Junior School, Birmingham

The Zoo

I want to go to the zoo,
Daddy, can I go with you?
Daddy, aren't the birds shy
Or is that just a lie?

Look, there's a bunny,
Doesn't it hop funny?
I saw a big fat nelly,
It was very smelly.

Daddy, there's a stripy horse.
Don't be silly, that's a zebra of course.
I saw a brilliant lion,
His name was Roary Ryan.

Daddy, look there's a monkey
Doesn't it look funky?
I saw a black and white bear
Panda, please take care.

I saw a massive snake
He was eating a piece of cake
I think I saw a marmoset,
Oh Daddy, can I have one for a pet?

But now it's time for us to go,
One last look at Dumbo.
I really love it at the zoo
Perhaps next time you can come too.

Mercedes Shelley (8)
Lyndon Green Junior School, Birmingham

Harvest

At harvest time we play lots of games
As we work up and down the lanes.
Harvest time is a time to share,
As balloons float in the air.

In the fields the corn dollies are made,
As the corn is being laid.
As the tractor rolls around,
The corn dollies lay close to the ground.

Emma Warwood (8)
Lyndon Green Junior School, Birmingham

Harvest

Harvest, harvest, corn growing in the fields,
The tractors moving their wheels.
Scarecrows scaring off the birds,
Corn dollies hanging on a line.
Food is growing,
Taking its time,
Celebrations, festivals, going on all night.
Fireworks bursting up, gleaming light.

All the giving and sharing,
Helping others like you.
When you are sleeping,
Others are eating.
Harvest, harvest, thanks to you,
People aren't starving.
Thank you.

Bethan Machray (8)
Lyndon Green Junior School, Birmingham

Senses

I see some bamboo as green as can be.
I hear a radio as loud as can be.
I smell some oil ready for seeds.
I touch a carpet as smooth as can be.
I taste an apple as sour as can be.

Sophie Simmons (9)
Lyndon Green Junior School, Birmingham

Why I Hate Mustard

I hate mustard
I'll tell you why
It's all hot and spicy
And makes me cry.

I hate it on sausages,
I hate it on chips,
It makes me drink water
In great big sips.

Sarah Hinckley (9)
Lyndon Green Junior School, Birmingham

My Little Sister

My little sister, she's only eight,
She's not the kind of sister that you'd want to hate.
She always seems so innocent - never, ever mean.
In five years she'll be thirteen.
Her lovely blonde hair, her smiley face,
Travel with her everywhere,
I think that she's ace!

Rebecca Jones (10)
Lyndon Green Junior School, Birmingham

Mums

My mum is cool,
She's very sweet,
She treats us fairly,
We all think she's neat.

There's one thing though,
That's a bit of a let-down,
Because, although she's cool,
She makes us go to school.

But other than that,
She's the best mum in the world,
But still,
I hate it when I go to school!

Emma Fitzgerald (11)
Lyndon Green Junior School, Birmingham

My Family

Dad will always be there,
To help me and Claire.
Mom will be there
To brush my hair.
My sis will be there
To be like a big cuddly bear.
My nan will be there,
To just be like my nan.

Rhiannon Satterley (10)
Lyndon Green Junior School, Birmingham

My Dog Ruby

I have a dog called Ruby,
She is my little gem.
Whenever I am upset,
She's such a cute pet.

She's 2 years old,
She's never cold
And the reason is
Her hair's so long.

It takes us hours,
To get her showered.
Then another two hours,
To groom her.

But I love my dog Ruby!

Lily Bennett (10)
Lyndon Green Junior School, Birmingham

A Disaster Holiday

A holiday in Cornwall,
Very nice, some would say.
But Dad took a tumble along the way.
'Do your shoelaces up,'
He would sometimes say,
But what else did I find along the way?
One lace undone and over he went
With a bump and a crash
His arm was all bent.
In a plaster and sling
And a tow truck for the car
Home we came, with our holiday gone
In just four days.

Stephanie Beech (10)
Lyndon Green Junior School, Birmingham

Danger

Danger is black and red.
It smells of toxic waste.
Danger tastes of slimy goo.
It feels so rough and bumpy.
So now I know when danger's coming
Argh!

Heather Pope (10)
Lyndon Green Junior School, Birmingham

Brothers

B rothers, brothers, brothers,
R yan is my brother and I hate him very much.
O thers love their brothers, but I definitely don't,
   I can't stand to touch him, I
T hink he smells as bad as a dirty dustbin.
H e makes me heave because he smells so *bad!*
E very day we have an argument.
R ows are all around the house.
S orry for you to read this, but overall I love him to bits!

Sophie Wills (11)
Lyndon Green Junior School, Birmingham

Georgia

G eorgia is my cousin, so infantile and sweet.
E verybody loves her and she has got small feet.
O thers want her, but they can't, they always have a
R ow over her.
G eorgia is cute but I am a lot cuter.
I love her to bits.
A ll is good and I love her like I should.

Molly Dewell (10)
Lyndon Green Junior School, Birmingham

Oh Jasper

Oh I do love my kitty, oh so, so sweet.
But when my dad found fleas crawling up his feet
We weren't happy, no, no, not at all.
We called him for his dinner
And now he gives us this.
Oh I do love you Jasper,
But I'm not giving you a kiss.

Emily Mansell (10)
Lyndon Green Junior School, Birmingham

Computers

Computers, computers,
I love computers,
Sometimes I think they even make me bonkers.

Computers, computers,
They even act as good as robots.
But sometimes they can be annoying
And make me want to break them.

Computers, computers,
Sometimes they're fun.
You can play games on your computer,
But that's only if you've got one.
So when you've read this poem,
Why don't you ask your parents for one this Christmas?

Bilal Ahmed (10)
Lyndon Green Junior School, Birmingham

Rainy Day

It's another rainy day,
Blowing troubles your way.
It'll be so boring,
Now Mum and Dad are snoring.

I wish it wouldn't rain,
The rain is such a pain.
My baby brother's crying,
I think I might be dying.

It's rain, it's plain,
I might prefer the cane.
It's rain that I hate,
It's rusting the gate.

There is nothing to gain,
With all of this rain,
But look, the sun's come out again.

Matthew Hoskin (10)
Lyndon Green Junior School, Birmingham

My Baby Brother

My baby brother's just a brat
And all I get is a whack.
He shouts all day and screams all night
He gets sympathy and then he smiles at me.

He gets his own way all the time,
He never leaves me alone.
He gets me wound up all of the time,
He never lets me be in peace on my own.
Just face it, my brother is a brat!

Jordan Bond (10)
Lyndon Green Junior School, Birmingham

My Mum

My mum is there for me when I'm down.
She works hard for me.
Her patience is lost easily.
There's no need to wind her up,
She'll shout and scream,
Her clothing sense is tops,
That's why she's my mum.

Lauren Gallagher (11)
Lyndon Green Junior School, Birmingham

My Life

My life is a total failure with everything I do.
I can't do anything but fall in goo.
I hate myself for what I have done
And I've just realised, my button is undone.

Daniel Hans (11)
Lyndon Green Junior School, Birmingham

Me And My Sister

Me and my sister are always fighting
But she never wins because I'm as fast as lightning.
There's not many fights that she has won,
Because I'm older than her and she acts like she's one.
She screams in the morning, she screams at night,
But still I'm always up for a fight.
Because she's always in Mom's bed with her dummy
Me and my sister.

Laura Russell (10)
Lyndon Green Junior School, Birmingham

Winter

Silver moon, glittering in the snow.
Windows iced-up like an ice rink.
Bare trees freezing their branches off.
Icicles hanging from lamp posts like
Leeches
    From
        Human
           Flesh.
Wrapped up people like ancient mummies.
Lakes shining like a silver fish.
Frosty breath like a train
Leaving its station.
Dusk falls as quick as a drunken sailor.

Danny Hawkins (10)
Perry Court Junior School, Bristol

The Cold

Winter moon, as silver as a fifty pence piece.
Vicious rain slams to the ground.
Hailstones fall like pearls from a pearl necklace.
Snow covering the ground as soft as a baby's teddy bear.
Bare trees freeze as the cold wind blows.
Icicles hang from the roof like darts.
Windows frozen like ice rinks.
Wind brushes past my face,
As if I am running the marathon.

Anna McDougall
Perry Court Junior School, Bristol

The Cold

Wrapped up people doddle around like baby penguins.
Icicles glow like fireflies.
Smoke blows out of mouths like a chimney.
Teeth chatter like hailstones hitting the floor.
Gardens lie with a soft blanket of snow over them.
Frozen lakes lay still like statues.
Dusk falls like a bullet.

Georgiana Carnevale (11)
Perry Court Junior School, Bristol

Cold

The smooth icicles are like long knitting needles,
Stabbing in the thin air.
The frosty puddles are as icy as a skating rink.
The snow blanketing the ground, like a duvet keeping you warm.
Hailstones pelting down at you, like bullets from a machine gun.
The snow is as soft as a handful of cotton wool.
Teeth chattering like a baby rattling its rattle.
The freezing weather is like a freezer door wide open.

Shannon Jenkinson
Perry Court Junior School, Bristol

Cold

Playground's covered in snow like a blanket covering a person.
People breathing smoke like a dragon breathing fire.
Frost is like a scarf covering windows and cars.
Hailstones fall from the sky like bullets from a gun.
The frosty moon shines like a silver coin.
Teeth chattering like people running in a race.
A layer of ice traps water like a bird in a cage.

Sophie Jackson (10)
Perry Court Junior School, Bristol

Come And Go Of Dusk

Dusk is creeping without a noise
The shining moon looks down on the Earth.
Freezing fish have steamy gills.
The lake is safe beneath an icy barrier.
The shivering wind runs like a bolt of frozen
Lightning.
Chattering birds have lost their voices,
Eerie coyotes howl with envy.
A beam of warmth strikes the land,
Sun is here,
Dusk
Is
Gone.

Nathan Rickard (11)
Perry Court Junior School, Bristol

White Wolf

The plague that is ice,
Creeps through the night
Like a pack of vicious hounds.
Its teeth are hazardous icicles
Red, not clear
For they skewer innocent rodents.
Its white fur is the merciless blanket of snow
That buries misguided insects alive.
Its razored claws are the lightning
That strikes the unsuspecting tree.
From this suffering comes
The only warm hope.

Ryan Perry (11)
Perry Court Junior School, Bristol

The Cold

Frost bites my hands like a vicious guard dog.
Trees bare like a naked man.
The soft snow is a blanket covering the floor.
Chattering teeth like glass shattering.
People puff smoke like a fireplace.
Ice shines like the silvery moon.
Water turns to ice as quick as a flash.
Fish freeze in the icy lakes.
Silky snow falling to the ground.

Kayleigh Blom (11)
Perry Court Junior School, Bristol

Licking Flames

Red and hot,
Shooting up,
Like a genie from a magic lamp,
Giving lots of light.
Your face getting hotter,
Turning shades of red *too!*

Flames licking you,
Like a ginger pussycat.
Warming, tickling you inside.
Everlasting energy,
Heat, light, entertainment
And a fire-breathing dragon!

The imagination . . .
Heating up my mind.
A campfire, on a mountain,
The painting of dawn.
The howling of dark wolves
Licking, flickering flames.

Bryn Tye (7)
Ridge Primary School, Wollaston

Hairy Object

Veg eater,
Loveable creature,
Naughty nibbler,
Silly giggler.

Crow hater,
Troublemaker,
Cage croucher,
Food cruncher.

Irritable itcher,
Silly scratcher,
Rambling roamer,
Happy stroller.

Cute character,
Dirty digger,
Hay chewer,
Master drooler.

That's my guinea pig.

Ross Blakemore (9)
Rosley CE Primary School, Wigton

What Am I?

Carrot muncher,
High jumper,
Cake scoffer,
Show topper,

Jump lover,
Muddy cover,
Rocking canter,
Will she scamper?

Wind galloper,
Should I wallop her?
Bumpy trotter,
Getting hotter,

Transition maker,
Hay raker,
Precise mover,
Lovely cruiser.

Sally Gate (11)
Rosley CE Primary School, Wigton

My Kennings Poem

Chocolate adorer,
Land explorer,
Telly flicker,
Lolly licker,

Welly wearer,
Cow carer,
Toilet hogger,
Hard slogger,

Tree feller,
Story teller,
Pop drinker,
Heavy thinker,

House keeper,
Heavy sleeper,
Fly hater,
Shed creator,

Early riser,
Always wiser,
Milk producer,
Sofa snoozer,

That's my dad!

Katie Rothery (10)
Rosley CE Primary School, Wigton

It's A Deadly . . .

Limb ripper,
Dinosaur killer,

Cliff leaper,
Territory keeper,

Two feeter,
Meat eater,

Cretaceous liver,
Terror giver,

Five 'tonner',
Slow runner,

Lizard king,
Monstrous thing.

It's a Tyrannosaurus!

Luke Williams (10)
Rosley CE Primary School, Wigton

Dolphins - Kennings

Squeak maker,
Human saver,
Water sprayer,

Shark killer,
Awe giver,
Eye grabber,
Fish snatcher,

Hoop jumper,
Crowd lover,
Nifty flipper,
Graceful swimmer,
Sudden vanisher . . .

Jonah Reid (11)
Rosley CE Primary School, Wigton

What Am I?

Trumpet maker,
Ear waver,
Tail swisher.

Water sprayer,
Dust bather,
Leaf eater,
Skin wrinkler.

Trunk holder,
Loud stomper,
Always together,
Big stampeder.

Ivory tusker,
Carries lumber,
Good rememberer,
Getting rarer.

Bianca Douglas (10)
Rosley CE Primary School, Wigton

Trouble Doer

Walk lover,
Annoys brother.

Cat catcher,
Ball snatcher.

Ankle nipper,
Sloppy kisser.

Long sleeper,
Toy keeper.

Drool spitter,
Eats litter.

Dirty pouncer,
Ball bouncer.

Father aggravator,
Food grater.

Book chewer,
Trouble doer.

That's my dog!

Christian Sellars (10)
Rosley CE Primary School, Wigton

Black Prowler

Black prowler,
Low growler,
Night walker,
Prey stalker.

Cat predator,
First rater,
Zoo feature,
Wild creature.

Lawrence Smith (10)
Rosley CE Primary School, Wigton

Sparkling Unicorns

Unicorns, with their horns sparkling so bright.
Galloping with their golden hooves,
Through the dark of night.

They sing while we are sleeping
And hide when we are awake.
I wish that I could see them
Oh please, for goodness sake.

I dreamt last night I saw them,
I was as happy as can be.
But then they started laughing,
When they looked at me.

Eleanor Stepaniuk (8)
St Joseph's Catholic Primary School, Bristol

Blue!

Think of something blue . . .
The sea and sky?
A whale with the most beautiful skin!
Ice is cold, you can feel it, I know it!
Blue is different, blue has light.
Blue is like Mother Nature, singing and dancing in the sky!
Blue is like a stream with ripples of gold.
Blue is so cold, when it touches your lips everything freezes!

Elena Bellavia (8)
St Joseph's Catholic Primary School, Bristol

Army Man Stan

Army man Stan
Doesn't need any medical van.

He sleeps with one sheet
Because he's the bravest of the fleet.

He never knew his dad,
That's really sad.

The loud sound of bombs, he cannot sleep,
Building trenches really deep.

He is my brother,
We love each other.

I fear to hear
That he has left here.

Liam Smith (8)
St Joseph's Catholic Primary School, Bristol

The Mermaid

She swims swiftly across the sea,
But not very loudly.
And she swings her golden hair
And cleans her chambered lair.

She likes to collect shells
And put them in her lair.
She'll play all day
And brush her golden hair.

She'll make the fish smile
And make the crabs jump.
She's never been in a trial,
Because she's got a great big smile.

Katie Riley-Fitzgerald (8)
St Joseph's Catholic Primary School, Bristol

Red

The sunset?
A juicy strawberry
Or a robin's red breast?

Red is a rose
Red is blood
Red is fire.

Red has a fiery temper,
Red is like apples,
Rosy-red cheeks,
Rudolph's nose
And Santa's clothes.
What is red?

Chelsea Dwyer (8)
St Joseph's Catholic Primary School, Bristol

In My Wardrobe!

In my wardrobe,
It is very messy,
'You should tidy it up,'
Said my aunt Tessy!

But I can't see what's the matter,
It's only stuffed with toys and clothes.
For instance my Game Boy
And the hat my mum wove.

Sometimes kids from school come over
And look around my room.
They ask me what's in my wardrobe,
I say, 'It's full of *doom!*'

So now you know what my wardrobe's like
And you should be aware.
But I still can't see what's the matter,
So I don't really care!

Priya Kaur (9)
St Joseph's Catholic Primary School, Bristol

Me An Mi Brother Kurtis

Me an mi brother beat up each other
An I always hit him first,
But then he punches me in mi leg,
But I still love him.

Bring it on brother, shut your mout,
Com on chase me brother,
I'll hit you, I'll hit you too,
But I still love him.

Den when his friend came,
They went straight on the trampoline,
I asked if I could go on,
He said no, but I still love him.

But now me an mi brother
Are like best friends,
But we still fight a lot,
But I'll love him forever.

April Henry (8)
St Joseph's Catholic Primary School, Bristol

Black

The night,
A deep dark well
Or a shark.

Black is smoke,
Black is dark,
Black is death.

Black has a big dark cloak.
Black is like arrows shooting.
Black is like a gun firing.

Black is like a skeleton rattling.

Mason Schwarz (9)
St Joseph's Catholic Primary School, Bristol

The Dreamcatcher

The dreamcatcher catches bad dreams, not good.
And frightens evil spirits away.
But when you wake up, you won't notice the power
That you are not haunted by in the day.

The dreamcatcher hangs at the foot of my bed,
Its feathers are as white as snow.
And, as if by magic, I start to feel
The bad nightmares are starting to go.

The dreamcatcher is mysterious
I don't know its name,
But it catches my bad dreams all the same.

Chloë Staples (9)
St Joseph's Catholic Primary School, Bristol

The Dog

There's a dog across the street,
He always eats meat,
He always tries to cheat.

He has a lovely voice,
Even though it's a bark
And he stays out in the dark.

He has a lot of soft toys,
And he gets out
With the boys.

There's a dog across the street,
He always eats meat,
He always tries to cheat.

Georgia Brain (8)
St Joseph's Catholic Primary School, Bristol

The Dream Keeper

The dream keeper is making dreams,
Using magic and fire beams.

The dream keeper waves his hand,
Making glitter fill the land.

The dream keeper wears a special hat,
With a pointy top and a magic cat.

The dream keeper has to fly high
And gives children dreams
And flies back to his dream house in the sky.

Zoe Boniface (8)
St Joseph's Catholic Primary School, Bristol

The Minotaurs!

The Minotaurs are coming,
Rumble, rumble, rumble, rumble,
They're all coming in an extremely big jumble,
Clash, clang, bang,
They're a terrifying gang.

They raise their axes 13 feet high,
I'm not being funny, it's not a lie
And then they charge, their horns quite large
Bing, bang, bong and my army's gone.

I'm the only one left,
I'm right by their chests.
They pick me up really high
And then I fly.
Ouch!

Alix Wines (8)
St Joseph's Catholic Primary School, Bristol

The Indian Brave

There once was an Indian brave
Who had ten thousand slaves.
He'd whip them and beat them;
He'd never once greet them
But now he is dead in his grave.

Rachel Emery (9)
St Michael's CE Primary School, Bristol

The Moon

The moon is like a piece of cheese
That has got a hole in it.
The moon is like half a face
The moon is the colour of custard
The moon is like a stone.

Toni-Lee Pope (10)
St Michael's CE Primary School, Bristol

The Magic Box

(Based on 'Magic Box' by Kit Wright)

I will put in my box . . .
The sight of snow on a cold winter's morning.
The sight of my family when we've won the lottery.

I will put in my box . . .
My dad laughing,
The splash of water.

I will put in my box . . .
The smell of my mum's perfume and clean sheets.

I will put in my box . . .
The sound of waves
The smell of stuffing.

I will put in my box . . .
A beach that will always have sun
And every day of my life.

Bethany Eveleigh (10)
St Michael's CE Primary School, Bristol

Six Ways Of Looking At A Puppy

A puppy is a fluffy ball
And its golden fur glistens in the sun.

A puppy is a teddy bear,
With a pair of glossy blue eyes.

Puppies are playful animals
And you can squeeze them night after night.

A puppy is a bar of melted chocolate,
You can dream of it all day.

A puppy is my dream,
That I could keep at the bottom of my heart.

A puppy is a tired-out animal,
When it has been playing all day long.

Molly Wardle (9)
St Michael's CE Primary School, Bristol

A Stranger Called This Morning

(Based on 'The Sound Collector' by Roger McGough)

A stranger called this morning,
dressed in black and grey,
put every colour in a bag
and carried them away.

The deep red of a broken heart
The grey of Grandma's hair
A ping-pong ball as pink as my cheeks
The green of a watery pear.

The cuddly white of a bouncy cloud
The black of a smelly bin liner
The blue of the blooming sea
The yellow of the gleaming sun.

The brown squishy mud
The runny red blood
The light-blue floods
The pretty pink card.

The purple of a purple dart
The hard brown wood
The *whooshing* cold flood
The beating heart.

Ella Sims (9)
St Michael's CE Primary School, Bristol

A Stranger Called This Morning

(Based on 'The Sound Collector' by Roger McGough)

A stranger called this morning,
dressed in black and grey,
put every colour in a bag
and carried them away.

The deep red of a broken heart,
The grey of Grandma's hair
A ping-pong ball that's as pink as my cheeks
The green of a watery pear.

The brown of a manky boot,
The purple of Grandma's legs
A whiteboard that's as white as a sheet,
Pink knickers hanging with pegs.

The orange from an orange,
The yellow of the sun
The violet of a Christmas card
The cream of a bun.

The gold of the goldfish
The blue of the bluebells
The silver of a shark
The green of a gill.

A stranger called this morning,
dressed in black and grey,
put every colour in a bag
and carried them away.

Scott Cousins (10)
St Michael's CE Primary School, Bristol

Stars

Stars are like Christmas lights,
Sparkling through the night sky.

Stars are like fireworks,
Exploding through the night sky.

Stars are like golden paper,
Reflecting through the night sky.

Stars are like the sun,
Lighting up the night sky.

Natasha Chadha (10)
St Michael's CE Primary School, Bristol

Toy Town

Maracas from Mexico
Bulls from Spain
Umbrellas from Scotland
When in comes the rain.

China dolls from Russia
A stick of rock from England
Footballs from Brazil
And penguins from Finland.

Jack-in-a-box from Poland
Onions from France
Rubber ducks from America
Argentina's doing a Latino dance.

Grace Boothman (9)
St Michael's CE Primary School, Bristol

My Box

(Based on 'Magic Box' by Kit Wright)

I will put in my box . . .
The smiling face of my nan
My mum, happy on her birthday
The laughter of a baby
And the sound of birds singing
The smell of chocolate pudding
The weather of Cyprus
And my dream to make it Christmas every day.

Lindsey Lloyd-Coleman (9)
St Michael's CE Primary School, Bristol

Six Ways Of Looking At Tinsel

Tinsel is a spiky snake that coils around your tree.
Tinsel is a shiny boa that wraps around your neck.
Tinsel is a vine hanging from your tree.

Tinsel is a piece of thread, long, shiny and proud.
Tinsel is a boa constrictor, long and beautiful.
Tinsel is a man, all different shapes and sizes.

Rebecca Higgins (10)
St Michael's CE Primary School, Bristol

Colour

(Based on 'The Sound Collector' by Roger McGough)

A stranger called this morning,
Dressed in black and grey,
Put every colour in a bag
And carried it away.

The red of a broken heart
The grey of Grandma's hair
A ping-pong ball that's as pink as my cheeks
The green of a watery pear.

The cuddly white of a bouncy cloud
The black of a smelly bin liner
The blue of the sea
The yellow of the gleaming sun.

The purple flying dart
The pink greeting card
The red beating heart
The multicoloured gum that's hard.

The red rose
The green tree
The blue water coming out of a hose
I wish I could climb a tree.

A stranger called this morning,
With no trace of a name
No one can ever have fame
With colours ever again.

Abbie Tuffin (9)
St Michael's CE Primary School, Bristol

The Sandy Air

The breeze of the sandy air,
The teasing of seagulls playing with someone's hair,
The smell of my mum's fudge cake,
The swishing from side to side
And the sound of the seagulls crying to each other,
The swish of the open breeze,
The squashing of the sand and shells.

Abigail Whittington (10)
St Michael's CE Primary School, Bristol

In My Box

(Based on 'Magic Box' by Kit Wright)

I will put in my box . . .
The crystal clear waves on a sandy beach
SpongeBob who's come to life
My first cuddly toy that I had when I was a baby.

I will put in my box . . .
The sound of a kitten miaowing
The sound of a barbecue on a Saturday night
The sound of my Game Boy with all the flashing colours.

I will put in my box . . .
The smell of salty, lush chips
The smell of a Chinese restaurant
The smell of a fresh duvet cover.

Harry Smith (9)
St Michael's CE Primary School, Bristol

Three Ways Of Looking At The Ocean

The ocean is like a massive swimming pool,
Welcoming all the swimmers.

The ocean is like an aquatic zoo,
With all the sea animals there.

The ocean is like a huge beast,
Gobbling up the sand.

Joe Alemzadeh (9)
St Michael's CE Primary School, Bristol

Sadness

Sadness is like the weeping cry from your one and only mum.
Sadness is like a rotting apple that has fallen from a tree.
Sadness is like a light-blue teardrop trickling down your cheek.
Sadness reminds you of the remembrance of your family.
Sadness is like the nightmare hidden in your dreams.
Sadness is like your pets in that moment of time.

April Buxton (10)
St Michael's CE Primary School, Bristol

A Stranger Called This Morning

(Based on 'The Sound Collector' by Roger McGough)

A stranger called this morning,
Dressed in black and grey,
Put every colour in a bag
And carried them away.

The silver of a shiny car,
The black of a computer screen,
The gold of the sandy beach,
The orange of a hot baked bean.

The white of the fluffy clouds,
The burning red of planet Mars,
The green of a juicy apple,
The brown of some Mars bars.

The pink of a chubby pig,
The golden burn of the sun,
The grey of a ping-pong ball,
The strange colour of a currant bun.

The deep red of a broken heart,
The grey of Grandma's hair,
A football that's as pink as my cheeks,
The green of a watery pear.

As gold as a goldfish,
The purple of Granny's legs,
As orange as an orange,
The bright blue bloomers on pegs.

A stranger called this morning,
He didn't leave his name,
Left us only colourless
Life will never be the same.

Ashley Davey (10)
St Michael's CE Primary School, Bristol

Fire

Waking up, his eyes are red with anger.
He gently hisses,
Smoking his orange cigar.
Slowly he creeps up to his victims,
Then he leaps, clawing at their skin.
They scream, their heads swaying,
He is dancing,
Seizing his victims,
Eating all in his path.
Pacing through the forest,
Savouring the taste of food.
His voice whispering death warrants,
Spinning, leaping, jumping.
He is slapped by his vicious wife,
Dampened down,
Dying.
The smoke is being dragged in,
He stops;
Lying in wait for next time,
When hunger strikes him again.

Peter Graham (10)
Victoria College Preparatory School, Jersey

The Putrid Potion

Thrice the speckled toad has croaked,
Thrice the raven has been stroked.
Round about the cauldron go,
In the magic potions throw.
Kill some bees,
Chuck in some fleas.
In goes water from the Fens,
One big turkey and some hens.
Snatch a tooth from a shark,
Don't forget they're very sharp.
Add to the cauldron
An elephant's chaudron.
Grab up a worm, let it squirm,
Chuck it in and make it churn.
Add the poison from a frog
Then the snout of a hog.
Throw in saliva from a cow,
Don't forget, you must know how.
Dung beetles should be chopped,
Rolling dung must be stopped.
In goes one big slippy snake,
Slide it in and let it bake.
Lower in a Chinese man
The man preferred is Jackie Chan.
Crumble in a giant horn,
The best is from a unicorn.
Then for the final terror,
One big golden eagle's feather.

Oliver Colston-Weeks (11)
Victoria College Preparatory School, Jersey

The Battle

As the ferocious battle rumbles loudly through the night,
Only to see deaths in this terrible fight.
As you hear the giant drum's last beat,
The camouflaged tank ploughs through on its metal feet.

The battle passes by, darkness and light,
To only see blood in this horrendous sight.
Hear the bombs' horrible roar
And the guns' loud bawl.

The cannonballs whistle through the smoky air,
A sound no man can ever bear.
Nobody knows what to do,
Apart from stand and do what they're told to do.

Harry Reid (10)
Victoria College Preparatory School, Jersey

Mountain

The monstrous mountain greedily grabs frost from the sky.
A ghostly haze lingers round the freezing clumps of sapphire sleet.
Misty clouds run and frolic about the snow,
The shivering ice clinging to them.
Crumbly moss crawling up the edge of chestnut-brown boulders.
Pine cones dive below them into the shade.
Emerald grass covering the land like a blanket of jade.
Sparkling water continues to tumble out of a stony spring.
Angered rocks run rampant down into the smooth valley.

Rowan Spencer (11)
Victoria College Preparatory School, Jersey

James' Deadly Potion

Throw in the head of a shark.
Which was cut up in the dark.
Now add a toe from a frog
And the nose off a dog.
Add a spike of a porcupine,
Then the potion will be fine.

Double, double, coil and boil,
Add some cod liver oil.

Add some skin off a snake,
In the pot, boil and bake.
Get the tooth from a rat
And the tail from a cat.

Put in the wing from a fly,
In the pot, boil and fry.
Tongue of newt, head of frog,
Hairy ear of a hog.

Sprinkle the tooth from a bat
And the whisker from a cat.
Grate in a dead swan's beak
And an old rotten leek.

Then we add a spider's foot
And half a bag of stolen soot.
Now we slice in an old seat
And we leave it for a week.

Now your potion's fit to kill,
Murder your enemy - it definitely will!

James Logue (10)
Victoria College Preparatory School, Jersey

Graveyard

The graveyard shivers in the moonlight, with death stalking its every
gravestone
As the trees whimper over the church's long-forgotten bells.
The headstones scream as the vines suck the strength out of them.
Spiders weave webs as the coffins rot with the bodies inside.
The ground quakes with fear as the gate swings aimlessly.
The bodies decay as the long centuries stride on.

William Millar (11)
Victoria College Preparatory School, Jersey

Haggis

I stagger into a café on a cold afternoon.
It's dark and dingy, but the only one in toon.
I study the menu and order haggis and chips
As I wait, I glance at the cooker, watchin' how the bacon flips.
The waiter brings it on a steaming hot plate,
The haggis looks like a piece of slate.
I give some time for my haggis to cool,
The paper in front of me, advertising a pool.
The waiter approaches, with gravy in hand,
My taste buds are jumping up and down like wind-whipped sand.
The haggis is literally exploding with glee,
Exactly the same feeling as me.
The haggis is given some gravy to help its strife,
And with a dance it springs to life.
Before I eat, I have a test - just to make sure it isn't processed!
As I give it a prod, it boogies with delight,
It gives thumbs up, which is a good sight.
I give it a whiff and it smells just grand, shame that it's as dry as sand.
Now there is the final test which separates the best from the rest,
My mouth is begging me to take a bite, but the haggis looks so tight,
Hard and round like a paper ball - that won't do, not at all.
I throw on another bit of gravy, the haggis starts singing, 'Give me
more baby!'
I pour it on and finish the pot,
The haggis bulges up and wiggles a lot.
I stuff it in my mouth and begin to chew, the smell is strong, 'Pee yew!'
It tastes lovely and my stomach begins to dance, first a leap and then
a prance.
It is so nice, I sing with glee, nothing could be happier than me.
And now I think of the other haggis' running in the hills,
Soon to become my evening dinner - with my afternoon pills!

Bradley Gibb (10)
Victoria College Preparatory School, Jersey

The Roar Of The Guns

The call of the drum sounds the advance,
the swords screech out of their scabbards.
Roaring like lions, the cannons boom, firing their doom into the gloom.
Muskets and rifles hammer and bang,
swords and bayonets clang, clatter and clash.
While the line holds, it spits out death at the advancing column.
The grass lies under a river of blood.
The hooves of the cavalry pound the ground into a muddy red pulp.
The sky burns orange, reflecting the fire of the battle.
Flames from the grass lick up to the sky.
Behind the lines, the trumpets wait for the order to retreat or to
advance.
The bugles sound the rush down the hill into the barricades.
The flags on the lances fly, flutter and flap,
just as the flags on the wall jump up high and fall down and die.
Then the cannons roar up again to hole the city wall,
the ladders shoot forward, ready to scale the mighty towers and
bastions.
But this is only one battle, there will be much more.

Fionn Douthwaite (11)
Victoria College Preparatory School, Jersey

The Storm

The ferocious thunder threw itself around,
All the way to homeward bound.
The wind smacked it a long way,
The thunder made sure it would pay.
When a big bolt of lightning came,
The wind bowed its head in sad shame.
Suddenly they heard a window smash,
As the hail started to thrash.
The wind thought about the tiles
And realised they had to go miles.
The rain sprinted down and made a flood,
Then that created a lot of mud.
The wind became so powerful it hit a tree
And that's when the shock came to me.
As I watched the branches snap,
I saw a pine cone bounding towards the trap.
As the snow came trembling down,
It hit the mud and had to drown.
In misery it turned into a terrible blizzard,
Then appeared a magical wizard.
He swished his wand and all was done,
He knew he had definitely won.

Cameron Stables (10)
Victoria College Preparatory School, Jersey

The Secret Garden

As the flowers whistle in the slight breeze,
Bluebells ring in the moonlight freeze.
Plants start to yawn before the sun sets,
Feeling tired because they haven't slept.
The pond sleeps silently as the moon
Peers from behind a dark brown tree.
The shed creaks slowly watching me
The greenish grass stares,
Swishing its leaves in delightful ease.
In the soil patch beyond the trees
Lies an ocean of many seeds.
The clouds which hurtle along the sky,
Gaze down at me with grateful sighs.
Screaming, screeching at the plants,
The wind bellows loudly in one big shout.
The fountain dribbles quietly,
Behind the shade of the silent tree.

Cyril Favre (10)
Victoria College Preparatory School, Jersey

The Sea

The waves smashing up on a sandy shore.
Rocks rolling onto the empty beach.
Boats hopping out of the wailing water.
Seaweed desperately clutching a rough rock.
Litter swimming in the shallows.
Seagulls staggering onto the salty sea.
Flying fish joyfully jumping out of the froth.

John du Heaume (10)
Victoria College Preparatory School, Jersey

The Forbidden Forest

As the trees whistle in the wind,
The leaves jump in the breeze.
The ivy creeps up the trunks of the trees,
Hugging them tight whilst it climbs.
It scrambles up the great mighty pines,
As the green grass slowly stretches beneath the vines.
Not a living creature in sight,
Nothing that can hurt or bite.
The forest sleeps in the cold, damp night,
Nothing moves . . . no, not one thing.

Jonny Falle (11)
Victoria College Preparatory School, Jersey

The Star

Slowly, silently, now the star,
Drives away in her Ferrari car.
All the way into outer space,
With lots of make-up covering her face.
Then once past the ozone layer,
She has to meet the goggle-eyed alien mayor.
As she flies fast past the red planet,
She stops off to buy gross green granite.
Having finished she has to pay
And says, 'I'll see you another day.'
When she has speedily entered the Earth's atmosphere,
She gurgles down a pint of Irish beer.
Back into her original home,
She has a tranquil bath of mostly foam.

Liam O'Regan (11)
Victoria College Preparatory School, Jersey

The Storm

Thunder and lightning run through the stormy skies,
Rain punches the dirty road.
Rubbish slides down the empty streets.
Tiles hit the cold floor.
Chimney pots trash the strong roofs.
Hail hammers on the damaged pavements.
Windows crash as they are smashed.
The hurricane strangles the nearby building.
Cars cartwheel over onto their flat backs.
Rough seas race along rocky beaches.
Shrapnel-like debris destroys hedges, plants and ponds.
Trees headbutt the muddy ground.
The wind beckons the terrifying tornado.
Destruction laughs at the horrendous ruins.

Frankie de la Cour (11)
Victoria College Preparatory School, Jersey

Battle

Black bombs whistle evilly through the air,
Cruel guns cry out as they are fired,
Death sneaks up on you,
While fire spits menacingly all around.
The smell of death lingers in the air,
Pain grabs you eternally as you die.
Bullets scream piercingly as they pass you,
Planes roar deafeningly overhead fighting an airborne battle.
Bayonets butcher their victims,
Tanks jump as they get hit.
No-man's-land gobbles up brave souls
And then the drum's last beat
Signals the battle's end.

Hugo Barette (11)
Victoria College Preparatory School, Jersey

Evil Sisters

In the kitchen cooking pot,
All the things that I have got.
In the cupboards, in the drawers,
On the shelves, in the stores.

In goes a pot of chilli sauce,
A bottle of wine and beer of course.
Malted vinegar, olive oil,
Milk and yoghurt, some old tin-foil.
Some mayonnaise, a glass of Coke,
Surely that'll make her choke.

In the bathroom, under the sink,
All different colours, blue and pink.
In goes a bottle of Mum's shampoo,
Some bubble bath and perfume too.

Dad's deodorant, lots of that,
Some purple liquid for the cat.
A block of soap, some mouthwash too,
Some toilet water from the loo.

Then outside, to the shed,
Some things in there that'll turn her red.
In goes sheep pellets, for curing sheep,
Surely that'll make her leap.

Some cow tablets, for an aching joint,
By now you'll surely get the point.
I don't like her, she's so mean,
I will laugh when she goes green.

It should turn to blue, next to brown
And hopefully sis'll gulp it down.
Then it'll smash her to a million bits,
All scattered around where sister sits.

Louis Sangan (10)
Victoria College Preparatory School, Jersey

The Battle

People dying everywhere,
Pure red blood flying anywhere,
Sadness, sadness falls on the muddy field.
Generals fuss as the bombs combust,
Snipers with their keen eyes,
Looking for where the evil enemy lies.
Bombs sprinting to the trenches,
Bullets shouting at the top of their voices,
Picking out an enemy of their choice.

Francois Thebault (11)
Victoria College Preparatory School, Jersey

Battle

Angry artillery vengefully throws shells into the battle,
Deadly bullets whistle wildly through the air.
Terrible tanks munch through the enemy troops,
Killer grenades blow away people for metres.
Rusty rifles spit bullets into the enemy's position,
Long-dead corpses slouched over the parapet.
Monstrous machine guns cut down all in front of them.
Helicopters viciously pummel enemy tanks.
Troops terrorise enemies with landmines.
Death is long overdue for even the best soldier.

Cameron Monro (10)
Victoria College Preparatory School, Jersey

The Great Battle

The bombs roared through the black sky,
Blood spat on petrified faces.
Flaming fire lit up the sky,
Buildings rolled over and crashed down into tiny pieces.
The creaking noise of the tank grew louder and louder, closer and
closer.
The machine gun's bullets sprinted through the air
Like birds running away when a loud noise has been created.

Struan Moore (11)
Victoria College Preparatory School, Jersey

The Battle

The bloody battle grumbles on
As the hail of arrows races furiously through the air.
The swords clash together
As their screams echo around the battlefield.
Iron balls are flung from the enormous canon.
The endless bullets of the guns sprint in every direction.
The moaning noise of the tanks
Drags through the dirty battlefield.

Jonny Singleton (11)
Victoria College Preparatory School, Jersey

The Beach

The wind whistles through my hair,
As the sea runs up the beach,
Pieces of rubbish rustling by my feet.
I listen and hear the crash of waves as they hit the walls,
The sky smiles down on everything.
The seaweed stands as still as can be
The shoreline throws out stones and pebbles,
Rock pools splashing playfully.

Joshua McGowan (11)
Victoria College Preparatory School, Jersey

My Car

The engine of my car coughs its way down the windy road.
The blaring music shouts out loud.
The wheels run like thunder down the motorway.
The horn wailing as it beeps.
The exhaust pipe chatters like a little bird.
The headlights stare at the darkness.
The wing mirrors jumping up and down,
Windscreen wipers wiping the rain away onto the road.

Luke Philpott (10)
Victoria College Preparatory School, Jersey

My Red Racing Car!

My red racing car is zooming,
Running along the track.
Its wheels racing in circles,
Thrashing the Ferrari.
The exhaust roaring ferociously,
Windows jumping up and down.
Headlights beaming brightly,
The engine screaming loudly.
Suddenly the brakes screech to a halt
Doors yawn open softly
Windscreen wipers swaying slowly in the pouring rain.

Dominic Hirani (10)
Victoria College Preparatory School, Jersey

Cloud

I amble along the sky,
The wind is pushing me,
Above the greenish ground I lie,
Everything I see.

I let out lots of water,
Upon the land and waves,
I return to my sky quarters,
More water's what I crave.

And when the wind stops pushing,
I hesitate and stop
And then I just lay lying
And drop some more raindrops.

And when I suck up some of the sea,
I have to run away,
The birds fly all around me
And then I stop and stay.

Tanguy Tomes (10)
Victoria College Preparatory School, Jersey

Clouds

He wakes up with his sleepy eyes
With the gorgeous horizon in front of him.
He glides swiftly through the air,
Muttering a tune through his jaws.
He gets battered by jets flying by,
But he just regains strength and carries on gliding.
He sees lots of wonderful sights under his misty feet.
He absorbs water and spits it out as rain.
He breathes in fresh air
Filling his lungs throughout the day.
He feels the strain under his sleepy eyes
And is tired by nightfall.
He goes to sleep at sunset.

Stephen Coelho (10)
Victoria College Preparatory School, Jersey

Fire

I dance through the cold nights, leaping and skipping,
Getting angry when people throw wood into me,
Making me growl and look menacing.
I glare, glance and stare at the people around me,
I cough and splutter as I skip and dance,
I grab and feed off the litter they throw into me,
I gaze at the black night sky.
I begin to sing in a crackly style,
My hair is golden-yellow, bright red and a hint of blue,
I am leaving a trail of black ash,
As the night wears on, I am beginning to die,
I feel cold and lonely, my body is shrinking,
Smaller and smaller until I am almost gone,
The people have left me to die in darkness, all alone.

Chris Minchington (11)
Victoria College Preparatory School, Jersey

Storm

As the wind whistles over me,
It howls, whines and frightens me.
The tree knocks and claws at the window,
With its strange fingers.

The rain cries down and hits
My strong fortress.
The thunder rumbles
Like a hungry stomach.
The lightning strikes,
Like a viper at his prey.

As the storm shouts,
I shout back,
It swallows me like a hungry boy.
I shiver and shut my eyes,
Wishing it could be over.

As the storm ends, it is as silent
As a schoolchild working.
Everything is calm,
Silent and peaceful.

Brad Morgan (11)
Victoria College Preparatory School, Jersey

River

As I sit by the river I hear so many things,
The water gurgles and swirls, doing a merry dance,
The waterfall rushes and runs and falls,
The water rages, crashes and shouts to the bottom,
As its water glistens in the colourful moon
And its voice whispers and echoes in the wind.
A mayfly swerves to avoid the rustling water,
A *pop* and a *clop,* and the mayfly is gone,
Further along she flows into the sea,
Still a part of you and me.

Graeme Overton (11)
Victoria College Preparatory School, Jersey

Chemicals

I fizz and buzz as the bubbles rise up,
I whistle and spout, banging and bonging,
I think I'm ready, gurgling and steaming.
I'm put to boil on that shelf of mine,
A little bit of this,
A little bit of that,
I'm turning green, whatever next!
I see men in white coats staring at me,
It's because I'm good-looking
Or something's wrong with me.
I look at my home, it's not much I guess,
But I try to think positive,
It's what's best,
For you and me,
Oh wait, no, no
Please don't drink me!

Austen Colback (11)
Victoria College Preparatory School, Jersey

Plane

When I wait in the hangar to be refuelled,
I cannot wait to get off the ground,
I sprint along the runway, charging at top speed,
Slicing through the sky and bursting through the clouds.
Rushing over land and hurtling over the sea,
When I fly low my deafening scream
Makes babies cry and car alarms wail.
During war I drop bombs while bullets bite me.
When I hit the ground I stick out my air brakes
While my tyres screech,
But for now I wait, dreaming, dreaming.

Cameron McLean (11)
Victoria College Preparatory School, Jersey

Mountain

I stand there, giant of my land,
Biggest of my friends.
I roll away stones when there is nothing to do
I giggle and shake with mirth,
When these funny little men try to climb me.
I cover the poor things in snow.
If they get to my tip they poke and jab me
With these funny things called flags.

I throw out clouds if they are full of rain,
But I don't mind snow.
I gaze down on the towns and wonder,
What's going on down there?

Now, what annoys me most
Is that their aeroplanes and helicopters always crash into me.
People mining into me for jewels - it is most frustrating
Can't they leave me alone?
Their machines chomp and guzzle my base,
Until they can go inside me.

I'm getting really angry,
They have gone too far,
My patience is at an end.
Finally I've decided the only way to get rid of them
Is to become a volcano.
Let's see how they like boiling lava.
Boom!
I squeak and squawk as the hot stuff pours down me.
No, I don't believe it . . .
These people are now studying me,
Saying things like *'fascinating'* and *'wow'*!
Will I never win?

Joseph Asplet (10)
Victoria College Preparatory School, Jersey

Football

The football whizzes through the air,
It soars through the grass
And smashes through the opposition's defence
And when it's really in the groove,
It ploughs past the keeper,
Into the back of the net.

When it goes off at half-time in the changing rooms
It gets loads of stick from both team managers,
Then it's in the middle of the tunnel,
Scared to death
As the players grit their teeth.
But when it is out there,
It is the real football!
Happy to roll in the mud.

It is not scared,
Only a little battered and bruised.
The football owner's name is being cheered by the crowd
Ever so loud!
Sometimes the football gets kicked so hard,
It flies to a cloud . . .
When it lands,
It is in the middle of the crowd.

George Minty (11)
Victoria College Preparatory School, Jersey

Darkness

The darkness runs over me,
Smirking as the light retreats
To the other side of the world.
He stoops over me,
Gazing at me all the time.
He plays with the moon,
Chit-chatting all night long.
He watches down below,
While all lights run themselves out.
He watches as the cars underneath him
Skip along the roads.
He screams as aeroplanes
Dance through his body of black.
He yawns as time walks by slowly.
He tires as his body of black
Runs out of energy.
He roars as the sun
Bursts through his last defences.
He retreats happily as he
Tiredly jogs back to his bed.

Robert Corfe (11)
Victoria College Preparatory School, Jersey

Leaf

I dance around to the music of the wind,
I still stick to my beloved home,
When I grow up I will leave my home,
I will be left alone to roam, roam, roam.
Now I will fall from the high sky,
Falling slowly, quickly, all different speeds,
I elegantly dance and swirl down,
Tumbling, tumbling to the weeds.
Because I have been trodden into the ground,
I have now joined a soily mound,
When it rains I will turn into mud,
But in the spring I will be soil for a spud.

Robert Cuming (11)
Victoria College Preparatory School, Jersey

Motorbike

The motorbike roars like a dinosaur,
Everybody will watch it race the other bikes,
The engine will make everybody jump,
If it squeaks, it will squeak in style,
If it is parked it will freeze,
So everybody will look at its beauty.

The motorbike will rule the town with its gigantic roar,
The motorbike can watch everybody and everything,
Its engine will keep running for weeks
The motorbike's energy runs out and it'll go to sleep,
But will wake up, full of action,
Again and again . . .

Rishi Gangaramani (10)
Victoria College Preparatory School, Jersey

Snow

I get thrown around by playful children,
I squeak and go everywhere when skis run me over.
I hug the window sills and lie on the rooftops,
I get blown around by the powerful wind
And get stuck in the spiky pine trees.
I feel warm when the sun is out
And I am compact and crisp under people's feet.
But I feel cold and lonely on a rainy day,
As I'm turning to mush.
I sit on the mountain peaks and stare at the sky
And gaze at the bottom of the mountain as skiers pass by.
I melt in the summer and glide down the stream.
I get scooped up in a bottle as I start to scream.
Then I get drunk or poured down the drain,
Now the whole process starts again!

Oscar Warr (11)
Victoria College Preparatory School, Jersey

Motorbike

I vroom and scream along the hard granite track,
If a friend goes past I growl at them.
If I am in the lead, I just turn and glance
And daydream of winning the cup.
My fat wheels sprint, sprint,
A quick pit-stop to eat and drink,
Out I go chasing, I'm out of breath,
When there is ten metres to go I chorus,
'We are the champions!'
I cross the line, my owner hugs me,
I am filled with joy,
Now I need to rest and have a sleep
The next race is waiting for me,
I can't wait!

Jamie Sunter (10)
Victoria College Preparatory School, Jersey

The Sea

I crash down on the shore as
I am ridden on by many people.
I never sleep, I'm always ready
Always pleasant and playful
But sometimes I'm blamed
For things I swear I didn't do
Like tsunamis, floods and tidal waves.

I'm like a playful cat,
Trying to get a string ball, getting people to play,
Just edging towards them.
I feel so lonely in the night,
No one to play with; no duvet to hug,
The only ones here are the fish
Who are so ungrateful and have never,
So far, thanked me for their home.

Sometimes in the night,
I howl and screech with the wind.
I used to be so big and wide,
Yet now I am so much smaller.
In the day I'm so lively
But in the night I just wash on the shore, quietly.

William Breeze (10)
Victoria College Preparatory School, Jersey

Leaves In The Breeze

The trees are swaying in the breeze,
The wind picks up the leaves
And drops them on the floor.
The wind comes running up,
Pushes the leaves along,
Has a breakdown at a wall,
Pushes and pushes until
It goes tumbling down the lane.
It gets caught in traffic,
Then swept up again,
It dances around
Without a care to spare,
Passes a river,
Picking up speed,
Hitches a ride,
With a garden seed.
Near its destination,
Swoops up into the air
It falls to the ground,
How did it get there?

Hugh Jennings (10)
Victoria College Preparatory School, Jersey

Fear

Fear is when you are frozen stiff,
Unable to move, unable to feel.
Fear makes your heart pound
Like an African drum.

Fear is like lightning striking
When you least expect it.
Fear makes your mind rush
Like a cheetah.

Fear is the second worst feeling
Right next to pain.
Fear is very, very bad
But all you need to fear is fear itself.

Alex Kennedy (11)
Victoria College Preparatory School, Jersey

Phoenix

It flies all day around the world
Healing the victims of others, with one single teardrop.

Its flame-tipped wings spread
As it gracefully glides above the world.

Its eyes sparkle in the sunlight like stars at night.
Then after its long flight, it settles on its perch
And is reduced to ashes to be reborn again for the next day.

Jack Helm (11)
Victoria College Preparatory School, Jersey

The Sea

The sea gnaws on the island's soft sand,
Like giant claws digging into flour.
The sea shouts, groans and moans,
Like a small creature dying slowly.
The sea is tough and rough
Like a lion killing its prey.
But the sea can be calm and gentle,
Like a small sleeping dog.
The sea is playful,
Like a cat with string.
The sea is beautiful,
Like a perfect painting.
The sea is part of me.

Ashton Vautier (10)
Victoria College Preparatory School, Jersey

Silence

The wind hammered against the windows, all day long.
We stared as the flames danced in the fireplace,
In the distance the waves slapped against the sand,
The kettle whistled in the kitchen,
Outside, the wind whispered in the leaves making them rustle
And then, there was nothing.

Sam Noel (10)
Victoria College Preparatory School, Jersey

Fear

I'm all alone on an eerie night,
Shivering and cold in the silver moonlight.

Fear is breathing down my neck,
Twisting my mind into a wreck.

My heart is pounding as I run,
Fear squeezes the breath out of my lungs.

My blood runs cold as fear attacks,
Freezing fingers scrape my back.

My stomach contracts and my throat pulls tight,
Fear engulfs me on this night.

Jamie Thorp (10)
Victoria College Preparatory School, Jersey

Lion - Kennings

A prey hunter
A blood taster
An aggressive animal
A fierce mammal
A sharp listener
A feast eater.
A lion.

Myles Wood-McGrath (10)
Victoria College Preparatory School, Jersey

The Sea

The sea shines with silver teeth,
Shining and gleaming,
With a royal blue face,
Drawing fishermen in
To its sharp, dangerous rocks,
Sucking them to their deaths.

As the sea bites into the shore,
It leaves its teeth marks
Of wrecks and bones on the shore.

Alexander Cornish (11)
Victoria College Preparatory School, Jersey

The Dog - Kennings

A carpet ripper
A fluffy bounder
A mischief maker
A shoe tugger
A cat chaser
A best friend
A room destroyer
A whirlwind wagger.

Samuel Hackwood (11)
Victoria College Preparatory School, Jersey

The Dog - Kennings

A shoe tugger
A scruffy bounder
A mischief maker
A carpet ripper
A best friend
A room destroyer
A mad wagger
A fish chaser.

Harrison Colley-Bish (10)
Victoria College Preparatory School, Jersey

The Earth

The Earth is big and round,
Spinning quietly round and round.
The only source of light is the sun,
It's big and bright.
There's no complex riddle
For it's hottest in the middle.
The equator is this place
The warmest smiley face.
Be careful, it's not always kind,
For the sun can fry the mind.
Maybe hope for water,
So Mother can have a daughter
And possibly a son.
Then Father's work is done.
The Earth is big and round,
Spinning quietly, round and round.

Thompson Fisher (10)
Victoria College Preparatory School, Jersey

My Perfect Fruit Bowl

A red apple,
A yellow banana,
A red cherry,
A green pear,
An orange orange,
A purple grape,
A silver bowl.

Andrew Tsang (10)
Victoria College Preparatory School, Jersey

The House Of The Dead

The darkness covers the room like a black blanket,
The floor creaks and the wind howls.
The moaning noises are from a ghost-like figure in a white cloak.
The dust scatters round the room, like feathers from a nest.
The webs made by spiders glow across the house.
From this day they say the house belongs to the dead.

Alex Wood (10)
Victoria College Preparatory School, Jersey

Peace

It sparkles in the sun,
Just like gold.
it brings us together,
It unites us.
It makes people become friends,
Peace is our friend.
Peace stops war.

Edward Pollard (11)
Victoria College Preparatory School, Jersey

Summer

The silent village sleeps,
In the summer sunshine.
As the boiling heat grabs me by the throat
Beautiful flowers jump from the soil.
As the sea eats up the beach I stare at the sun
It dances an ugly dance in my head
That's summer for you!

Sam Bowen (10)
Victoria College Preparatory School, Jersey

Fear

It was a dark gloomy night as the moon enveloped the world in its darkness.
The sting of fear struck him like a dagger in the back.
He could hear the deafening sound of fear coming towards him.
He was so terrified he couldn't even speak.
His hands shook like a tree in the wind.
He could feel his demise coming closer and closer.
The fear made him shrivel up like a prune.
He could taste the sharp, sour taste of fear in his mouth.
Suddenly he saw a large figure emerge from the shadows.
He closed his eyes waiting for death to come.

Samuel Allen (10)
Victoria College Preparatory School, Jersey

Fear

Whoosh! The trees rustled
As if they were rickety chairs.
Darkness enveloped its dark velvety cloak
Around the world,
As the stars sprinkled their tiny shiny sequins
Upon the world
I looked out of my window
Rats scurried by looking malicious
My heart pounded like a church bell,
My door creaked, I was scared,
Fear took over my taste buds,
My heart split like a saw through wood,
The wind slapped me in the face,
Fear was here to stay.

Luke Chinniah (10)
Victoria College Preparatory School, Jersey

The Swan

A feather quilt
A water mover
A smooth silk
A swift swimmer
A bread eater
A swimmer's life
A great diver
A ferocious yapper.

Thomas Harries (11)
Victoria College Preparatory School, Jersey

Robin Hood

Here, underneath this little stone
Lies Robert, Earl of Huntingdon.
No archer was as good as he,
And people called him Robin Hood.
Such outlaws as he and his men
Will England never see again.

Kimi Shinh (9)
Wolf Fields Primary School, Norwood Green

My Funny Brother Drue

My funny brother Drue,
He is as sly as a snake,
He cracks a joke to make me laugh,
That's why he's my favourite.

My funny brother Drue,
Is nice to me half of the time,
When I was small, my brother always stood up for me
And he still does.

My funny brother Drue,
Is really good at console games,
That's why he teaches me to play them
And when I get stuck I go to him.

My funny brother Drue,
Sometimes locks me in my room
And sometimes doesn't let me in his,
Even though the PS2 is in there.

My funny brother Drue,
Is sometimes really moody
And sometimes hits me,
So I hit him back.

My funny brother Drue,
Is mostly nice to me
And helps me with my homework,
When my mum is busy.

Floris Atkins (11)
Wolf Fields Primary School, Norwood Green

Untitled

The fairy has hope,
She can cope,
Her bells go,
Ding, dong, ding, dong.

Her clothes are like shiny stars,
With golden flowers,
Her sparkly wand glimmers like a star,
Tinkle, tinkle, tinkle, tinkle.

She is sweet like candyfloss,
She acts like a drama queen,
She eats sweet candy, but not every day,
She is very sweet, like a soft blanket.
In the blue and grey sky.

Hirali Ganatra (10)
Wolf Fields Primary School, Norwood Green

My Granpa

His smile is like a floating angel, high in the sky.
His hair's sparkly like silver twinkling in the night.

He's as thoughtful as the sun shining upon us.
He is kind, like when an angel is flying through Heaven.

So without you, it would be like December without Christmas.

Anusha Bhamm (11)
Wolf Fields Primary School, Norwood Green

The Devil
(Inspired by 'I Met at Eve' by Walter de la Mare)

I met at dawn the Devil at work,
He had a hot and evil face,
Filled with cold laughter of his other victims
He dragged me down to the Valley of Darkness.

He smirked at me when I silently cried,
I tried to hide my fear of darkness,
But his power over me made me cry even more,
His heart of stone told me to work.

As I grew powerless from his laughter,
The Angel of Hope came in an instant,
Its powerful light swept darkness away,
It showed me my past, present and future.

I met at dawn the Devil of work,
He had a hot and evil face,
Filled with cold laughter of his other victims,
He dragged me down to the Valley of Darkness.

Gaurav Sood (11)
Wolf Fields Primary School, Norwood Green

Weekdays

On Monday I went to get some meat
Sitting on my car seat, I found some meat.

On Tuesday I went to get some soap
I found my friend and said, *'Ho! ho!'*

On Wednesday I had some fun,
I went to the market and bought a yummy bun.

On Thursday I played with my buddy,
It was such fun because I won.

On Friday I danced so much,
So did my friend, whose hand I did touch.

Naneesh Bhathal & Saira (8)
Wolf Fields Primary School, Norwood Green

Best Friends

My best friends always play with me
My best friends always help me
My best friends are always kind to me
My best friends are always happy
My best friends are always there for me
My best friends always stick up for me
My best friends always stay with me
My best friends are my best friends!

Amandeep Sidhu (9)
Wolf Fields Primary School, Norwood Green

Dolphin Daze Dashing!

When you see a dolphin dashing up high
And back in the water again
In, out, in, out
You can make friends with the dolphins
And have a good swim.
When the dolphin goes to sleep,
You can see the sunset
And hear the dolphins squealing
That's what you call a
Dolphin's dream!

Heather Beaman & Kayciann (8)
Wolf Fields Primary School, Norwood Green

Best Friends

I like to play
Just in May.
Heather Beaman is my mate,
We arrive at school so very late.

I like bananas
She likes piranhas.
I hate dogs
And she hates frogs!

We are the best, for ever and ever
Together we are so very clever.
I like to quiver
She likes to shiver.

So much the same,
We are, aren't we?
We'll shoot to fame,
Just wait and see!

Jogita Dari (8)
Wolf Fields Primary School, Norwood Green

Bad Crime

Me and my parents have a good life
Then I think about the people who get killed by a knife.
All these killers; they're not so good,
The people thought they had a nice neighbourhood.

All these killers think they're very cool
Then they go out and use a dangerous tool.
When the killers drink a lot of whisky,
They don't know they're doing something risky.

When these people think they look cool,
I just think they are being big fools.
When these people break people's knees,
All I know is they mean nothing to me.

Rishi Kotecha (9)
Wolf Fields Primary School, Norwood Green

No Word Of A Lie

I have Einstein's brain and that's
No word of a lie.
I can climb Mount Everest in one second and that's
No word of a lie.
I can beat Kelly Holmes in a race and that's
No word of a lie.
I can go round the world in one hour and that's
No word of a lie.
I can turn into any animal and that's
No word of a lie.
I have super powers and that's
No word of a lie.
I can eat ten thousand apples in one second and that's
No word of a lie.
I can drown and survive and that's
No word of a lie.
I can freeze and won't feel cold and that's
No word of a lie.
You don't believe me do you?
All right, all right, all right,
I'm the biggest liar in my school and that's
No word of a lie.

Rivar Hart (9)
Wolf Fields Primary School, Norwood Green

My Teacher

I have a teacher who is always moaning
And never stops groaning.

She expects us to do well
Or she will tell.

She is as kind as my mum,
She does a music lesson and expects us all to come.

The lessons are so long and boring,
Half the class are snoring.

After school is the best,
Because it's the only time we get to have a rest.

The next day we end up having a test.

My teacher is a star,
But sometimes she goes too far.

Davina Thiara (9)
Wolf Fields Primary School, Norwood Green

I Met At Eve

(Based on 'I Met at Eve' by Walter de la Mare)

I met at eve the princess of dreams,
Her skin as white as snow.
Her hair flowing like a gentle river,
A big golden crown on the top of her head.

Her eyes were dim in the moonlight,
As she tiptoed in her delicate slippers.
Her lilac gown walking behind her,
In the cold breeze.

Her lips as red as roses,
As the moths shine in front.
The cold breeze calls 'goodbye',
As she sings a lullaby.

Her cottage is right at the top of the mountains,
With great misty walls.
As she tiptoed to her cottage,
There was no cottage to be found.

Her voice had been echoed,
As the owls' wings were silent.
Nothing else could be heard,
Just birds singing lovely tunes.

I met at eve, the princess of dreams,
Her skin as white as snow.
Her hair flowing like a gentle river,
A big golden crown on the top of her head.

Sabah Malik (10)
Wolf Fields Primary School, Norwood Green

I Met At Noon

(Based on 'I Met at Eve' by Walter de la Mare)

I met at noon,
The princess from the moon,
Her golden hair flowing behind her
As she walked along in her delicate slippers.

Her lips as pink as the evening sky,
Her skin as white as snow.
Her eyes glittering in the starlight,
A wreath of roses upon her head.

As she flies high,
Into the sky.
To meet her friend Venus,
Who sits on the throne of love.

Down below on Earth,
She wanders through the valleys.
Looking closely at each stream,
To see her reflection beam.

I met at noon,
The princess from the moon.
Her robes fluttering behind her,
As she walks around in her delicate slippers.

Ravinder Kallha (11)
Wolf Fields Primary School, Norwood Green

FA Premier League Clubs!

Arsenal won the FA Cup,
In 2005 they went shooting up.
I saw them play against Man U,
They won the match 3-2.

Chelsea are practically the best,
In a second they beat the rest.
They have amazing skills and touches
And leave the opposition using crutches.

Liverpool are believed to be the best,
In all of the west.
They won the European title,
Which was very vital.

Manchester United always win,
The other team stands on the brink of a pin.
Ryan Giggs took a free kick,
He had done a perfect trick.

Newcastle bought Owen from Madrid,
They didn't realise he's just a kid.
Newcastle took the first kick
And in five minutes Owen scored a hat-trick!

Tavleen Grill (11)
Wolf Fields Primary School, Norwood Green

My Brother The Lion

My brother the lion,
Has got black curly hair
He's got brown eyes
And likes to eat pears.

My brother the lion,
Is a very naughty boy
He acts silly all the time
And likes to play with toys.

My brother the lion,
Is as fat as my dad
He weighs a lot more than me
And I'm older, but he's bad.

My brother the lion,
Always wears his red shirt
But at the end of the day
He gets it covered with dirt.

My brother the lion,
Acts very tough
But when he shows it
My mum's had enough.

My brother the lion,
Has black curly hair
He's got brown eyes
And likes to eat pears.

Kavita Sharma (11)
Wolf Fields Primary School, Norwood Green

My Big Sister

My sister's like a gentle robin
She cheers me up whenever I'm sobbing
Whenever I see her,
I get excited.

My sister never gets in trouble
And she is soft as a bubble.
But then I saw in my dream,
Me and my sister eating ice cream.

She has a very sweet voice
Whenever she speaks I have no choice.
Then after a while,
She built me a smile.

One month had passed,
But I found that out very fast.
And I didn't know I grew
But from then, my sister and me were new.

Karanvir Singh Attwal (11)
Wolf Fields Primary School, Norwood Green

Snow

(Based on 'I Met at Eve' by Walter de la Mare)

I met at eve, the princess of snow,
She has white curly hair,
Which flies behind her wings,
Her eyes are as blue as the summer sky.

She lives in the clouds above,
Coming down every winter for the snow,
For her chilling breeze,
We hear the rustle of the trees.

She wears a long cloak, as white as teeth,
Her trousers as long as a giant,
Her shoes as gleaming as diamonds,
Her skin as white as a ghost.

Her nose is as small as a button,
Her lips as red as blood,
Her weight as light as a feather,
Her personality as bright as the sun.

Her crown is made of ice,
Which shimmers in the moonlight
Her rings that shine in the starlight,
That is made from blue sapphires.

I met at eve, the princess of snow,
She has white curly hair
Which flies behind her wings,
Her eyes are as blue as the summer sky.

Karmpreet Kaur Heran (11)
Wolf Fields Primary School, Norwood Green

The Silly Clown!

One day I went to a circus,
I saw a clown called Mircus.
Then he did a funny trick,
By picking his nose and flicking it.

He ran into the brick wall,
While he was playing football.
He jumped in the crowd
And then he shouted, 'Bogies,' out loud.

He called his girlfriend Fircus,
To come and join him in the circus.
She said she had come from Dover
And then, at last, the show was over.

Deep Singh Bedi (10)
Wolf Fields Primary School, Norwood Green

My Mum

My mum is as soft as a smooth blanket.
She is like a beautiful butterfly.
She still has her jewellery casket,
Everyone still hates the housefly.

Whenever she is angry,
She is a blazing fire.
Her hair is so beautiful,
She doesn't even need a hairdryer.

Whenever she is worried,
She is as beautiful as a red rose
And also, whenever she is worried,
She is as gentle as a newborn baby.

Whenever she feels lonely,
I feel like crying.
But whenever she is near me, I cannot cry,
But the only thing to do is pray.

Akhila Pakalapati (11)
Wolf Fields Primary School, Norwood Green

Colour Poem

Red is like a roaring flame,
Red is like a hot game.
Blue is like a wavy sea,
Blue is like the sky, facing me.
Green is like the evergreen grass,
Green is like the wind rushing past.
Orange is like the sun setting down,
Orange is like a queen's crown.
Black is like a shot of lightning,
Black is like two people fighting.
Pink is like a packet or roses,
Pink is like a pocketful of posies.
White is like a fluffy cloud,
White is like a child, singing out loud.
Yellow is like a beehive's honey,
Yellow is like a big pot of money.
Brown is like a grizzly bear,
Brown is like the colour of my hair.
Purple is like the smell of lavender,
Purple is like the colour of my calendar.
Peach is like the look of a beach,
Peach is like a soft smooth cheek.
Aqua is like a swimming pool,
Aqua is like a person acting cool.
But overall I have a favourite
And guess what it is?
All of them!

Zoé Chopra (10)
Wolf Fields Primary School, Norwood Green

The Meeting At Dawn

(Based on 'I Met at Eve' by Walter de la Mare)

I met at dawn, the angel of light,
Beautiful face, peaceful place.
Birds tweeting like a sweet melody,
Trees rustling in the calm air.

Angels floating like balloons,
Flying high in the deep blue sky.
Their wings fluttering like a butterfly,
Like a tranquil harp that's what they are.

Their hair as golden as precious buttercups,
Their gentle voices like part of the sounds of nature.
Their eyes so bright, shining like light,
Moving swiftly, it's hard to catch them in sight.

Gripping a wand which controls evil,
A wand working for peace, amongst the people.
Sparks of magic, like shooting stars,
Watch them soar across the velvet blanket.

In the secluded woods, angels dwell,
Living in treetops, from which they propel.
To quickly reach us, to help us
In our time of need.

I met at dawn, the angel of light,
Beautiful face, peaceful place.
Birds tweeting like a sweet melody,
Trees rustling in the calm air.

Harveer Sandhu (11)
Wolf Fields Primary School, Norwood Green

My Brother . . .

My brother's hair is as spiky as a hedgehog's
Going out at night and attracting the girls.

He is as strong as the mighty King Kong
Knocking me out, when I say, 'Time out!'

He is as helpful as a butler, cleaning up the house
Serving drinks and taking out the trash!

He's as nice as the morning sunshine, jumping up and down
Always laughing at my jokes as though I was a clown!

Without him

I'd be as bored as a roller coaster without any movement,
I'd be as lonely as the last leaf on a tree!

Gavin Singh (10)
Wolf Fields Primary School, Norwood Green

Night!

Night is like a clown,
Scaring me with his evil laugh.
He chases me non-stop,
Until he gets me and slices me in half.

Night wears a black cloak
And carries an axe.
His chest and legs are skeleton bones
Made out of disgusting snacks.

His face is full of evil,
His eyes are full of blood.
He likes to eat the flesh of people,
He has an afro made of mud.

Night floods the Earth with darkness,
He's super-fast, you can barely seem him.
He comes in your dreams and kills you,
When you die, you see a light so dim.

Sarandeep Gill (10)
Wolf Fields Primary School, Norwood Green

My Mum And I

She is always in my heart,
She is always in my sight,
Without her I am a moon without craters,
Orbiting through the night.

She is as nice as an angel,
Flying in the sky
She is very pretty,
She also is shy.

She is so beautiful,
She is so pretty,
She is so lucky,
She lives in London city.

This is very true,
We are best friends,
We get much closer
And our friendship extends.

She is the best mum
In the entire world,
Her hair is kind of straight,
Not that curled.

She is always in my heart,
Always in my sight,
Without her I am a moon without craters,
Orbiting through the night.

Noor Vijay (10)
Wolf Fields Primary School, Norwood Green

My Brother

My brother's as strong as the mighty Kong!
Knocking me out, even when I say, 'Time out!'

He's as happy as the trees, giggling at each other,
Laughing all around, jolly when he's near his brother!

As sweet as the morning sunshine, jumping up and down,
Always laughing at my jokes, as though I'm some kind of clown!

Faster than Shoad Akhtar and Brett Lee,
Zooming to catch his food, as though he is some sort of bee!

I'd be as July without summer,
I'd be as bored as a roller coaster without any movement!

I'd be as sad as the sky when it cries,
I'd be as inactive as a cheetah without its legs!

Haroon Aslam (10)
Wolf Fields Primary School, Norwood Green

The Whale In The Thames

In the Thames there was a whale,
She was as bright as the sky.
>   *Amazing!*

People cheering awfully loud,
Confusing the whale a great deal.
>   *Fear!*

At night the whale was sad,
Still searching for her family.
>   *Lonely!*

In the morning, people were sad,
Looking at the whale on the ground.
>   *Oh no!*

The people saved the whale,
Yeah! Yeah! Yeah!

They were taking the whale out to sea,
But unfortunately, she died.

Anas Chemmach (10)
Wolf Fields Primary School, Norwood Green

The Beautiful, Sad Whale

W hale in London
H owever did it come here?
A wesome
L ovely
E veryone cheered

I t was so sad
N ever felt so lonely, like a bird in the sky

L ooking for deep water
O n the beached ground
N eeds its mother desperately
D oesn't know how to get home
O n a rescue boat
N o chance of surviving.

Mujib Mustafa (11)
Wolf Fields Primary School, Norwood Green

The Whale Who Was In London

I saw a whale in London,
It looked so big.
Everyone saw it swim,
Past London Bridge.

The whale felt lonely,
It looked so hungry.
It saw a fish,
Past London Bridge.

The whale was sad,
It wanted to play.
It just wanted to go,
Past London Bridge.

Poor baby whale,
So alone in the Thames.
Just wanted to go home,
Past London Bridge.

In the news, we saw the whale, dead,
Everyone burst into tears
And ran off,
Past London Bridge.

Luck Deep Bains (10)
Wolf Fields Primary School, Norwood Green

A Whale

I saw a whale in the River Thames,
Separated from its pod.

It was as lonely as the last leaf left on a tree,
As scared as a rabbit in the headlights.

I saw a whale in the River Thames,
Separated from its pod.

Like a giant blue submarine, with no water to swim in,
Like a stranded Eskimo in the North Pole.

I saw a whale in the River Thames,
Separated from its pod.

It was as strange as a polar bear in the Sahara Desert,
As sad as a child with no friends.
But now it's gone.

Christie Self (10)
Wolf Fields Primary School, Norwood Green

The Whale

I'm lost in London
It was a grey and rainy day
Excited as a squirrel finding a nut
There's a whale in London.

I was curious
I was confused
Amazing, incredible
There's a whale in London.

The tide was out
I was alone
I was as scared as a far planet from the sun would be,
There's a whale in London.

I needed help
I wanted hope
I needed water
There's a whale in London.

My tail didn't move as much
I felt all warm
And then everything went pitch-black
There *was* a whale in London.

Harinder Ahluwalia (10)
Wolf Fields Primary School, Norwood Green

There's A Whale In The Thames!

Wow! I can't believe it,
A whale! A whale in the Thames.
It is so big, like a submarine,
So many people here to see it.

Children, men and women, all here to see,
A whale! A whale in the Thames.
Everyone pointing at the huge sight,
But everyone wondering if it is safe.

Night falls and it's still floating in the water,
A whale! A whale in the Thames.
It is cold and the whale looks tired,
Everyone is now worried about it.

By the morning the huge whale lies on the bank like a stranded ship,
A whale! A whale in the Thames.
Now it is stuck and needs help,
Children cry and rescuers arrive.

They all arrive, boats, helicopters and tugs, all here for
A whale! A whale in the Thames.
They work together to get the whale onto the tug,
It is now on, maybe they can get it back to the sea in time?

Oh no! It's too late, the whale is dead,
No whale! No whale in the Thames anymore.
Everyone is sad, but they tried their best to save it,
I hope this was the first and last whale in the Thames.

Neha Gohil (11)
Wolf Fields Primary School, Norwood Green

Poor Baby Whale

My poor baby whale, all alone.
No one beside him to comfort him.
He does not know what to do
He doesn't know where to go.

My poor baby whale, all alone.
He is worried stiff and doesn't know where to go.
He doesn't know what to do
I wish I could look after my baby whale.

My poor baby whale, all alone.
Everyone staring at him, he's by himself.
He went down the wrong channel
And I lost my poor baby whale.

My poor baby whale, all alone.
At night he has to sleep by himself.
I wish I could look after my baby whale,
My baby wonders where I am,
I wish I could show him,
Where's my poor baby gone?

Aaron Bhangu (11)
Wolf Fields Primary School, Norwood Green

My Mum

M y, my, my,
Y ou can see

M um's great, she can do anything
U ses saltwater on icy patches, *brrr!*
M ums can squeeze you till you give them a hug

I n the morning she will bring you tea
S ometimes she's an angry mum

C ause my mum is cool
O i!
O l!
L eave my son alone she says
    That's my mum, I love you!

Deepinder Jay (11)
Wolf Fields Primary School, Norwood Green

Night

Night strikes
Death!
Through your soft, delicate *heart!*

Night is like an alley
Mysterious and frightening,
It's a determined
Lightning!

Night eyes are the stars
Shining and keeping an eye on
You!

Night is a deadly Ninja
Coming to create havoc across the
World!

Night wears a dark black cloak,
With death all over it and pitch-black buttons.

Night is swift like a brutal cheetah in a deadly jungle.
Night's face is made of souls he has killed!
Night lives in the depths of Hell.

Deserted and mysterious night is . . .
Deadly!

Harveer Jutla (10)
Wolf Fields Primary School, Norwood Green

Whale In London!

What can you see?
I can see people crowding
Excited like they've seen a shark,
I can see people jumping in the water and swimming towards me
Petrified!

What can you feel?
I can feel my organs being crushed
I can't breathe, it's like someone's put a paper bag over my head.
I'm feeling isolated
And I want to see my mum and my family.
Lonely!

What can you hear?
I can hear people screaming like they're being eaten,
Others are cheering and it's confusing me.
I can hear machines moving closer and closer
And I can hear my mum yearning for me.
Scared!

I'm moving closer out to sea,
My mum is still yearning for me,
My eyes are closing, I cannot breathe,
My eyes are shut now, I have to leave.
Dead!

Raminder Bhathal (11)
Wolf Fields Primary School, Norwood Green

Life

There is no armour for us to wear,
No wall or fortress we can build,
No strength to help, no shield for fear,
To equal what the heart has willed.

Life is tough, life is hard,
Who can protect us when something's wrong?
People crying, people dying,
For everyone knows life isn't long.

Death for death, tears for tears,
Why can't all of the world be friends?
Why can't we forgive and forget?
Make the most of your life, before it ends . . .

It's so sad when someone dies,
But . . . hey, it's natural,
It's part of life.
At least you'll go to a better place
Where you will be treated
With great care . . .

Lucinder Kaur Sandhu (10)
Wolf Fields Primary School, Norwood Green